The Pasta SAUCE Collection

Printed in the United States of America

For inquires contact:

PASTA HOUSE
P.O. Box 4120
Carlsbad, CA 92018
1-800-795-2512

Table of Contents

Table of Contents

Chapter 3

Chapter 4

Chapter 5

Table of Contents

A Word About Pastas and Their Sauces

Pasta is probably the most versatile of foods. It is made into literally thousands of variations around the world. But the secret of pasta's variety isn't just in the many different shapes. By far the greatest variety in pasta dishes results from variations of the sauce or topping used to add flavor to the pasta. And even if we focus on primarily European variations, the choices are still too numerous to count.

In this book, we have collected a virtual buffet of tastes and styles, for healthy appetites and light eaters; for those with simple tastes, and those with a passion for the exotic. Indeed pasta pleases everyone. A five-year-old with spaghetti and meatballs is enjoying his supper every bit as much as a dinner guest savoring truffles in wine sauce.

Pasta is unique in that it works just as well with rare or exotic ingredients, such as smoked eel or caviar, as it does with an economical sauce of tomatoes and seasonings. By choosing the right sauce, you can make a meal suitable to serve someone's boss, perfect for neighborhood kids, or fast and delicious for a hungry worker. You can make pasta a first course, side dish, or main event.

Pasta is not only versatile, appealing, and time-saving, it is also good for you. Pasta, along with bread, cereals, and vegetables, are complex carbohydrates (as opposed to simple carbohydrates, like sugar). Complex carbohydrates take longer to digest than simple carbohydrates, so they are very satisfying to eat—you need to eat less to feel full. A diet rich in complex carbohydrates is usually low in fats, provides sufficient protein, and ample vita-

mins and minerals. It is the sort of diet that fuels marathon runners and satisfies dieters (with the right sauces); it is a good choice no matter what your special dietary needs are.

Most pasta sauces can be made in comparatively little time. While some sauces can be whipped up in only a few minutes, even the ones that must cook slowly don't require that much actual preparation time. While the sauce simmers and fills your house with cooking smells, you can be off doing something else.

COOKING PASTA

Pasta should be cooked in lots of boiling water. Although you might do with less water than what is recommended, which usually means using a stock pot or large kettle, you'll at least need a large pot which holds 4 to 4-1/2 quarts for cooking one pound of pasta. Fill the pot to three-quarters of its capacity. Add salt and bring the water to a boil. Adding a little oil to the water helps to prevent it from frothing on the surface and boiling over rapidly. Cooking in too little water will cause the noodles to stick together regardless of how much oil you may add to the water. When the water has reached a rolling boil, add the pasta, a little at a time, then stir it slightly and let the water return to a boil. Be ready to reduce the heat, to prevent it from boiling over.

Cook fresh pasta anywhere from 15 seconds to 3 minutes. Dried pasta takes between 2 and 12 minutes depending on shape and thickness. Time your

sauce so that it is ready when the pasta finishes cooking. The pasta will become soft and gluey if it waits too long.

DONENESS

When cooked, the pasta should be firm yet tender, or *al dente* (literally "to the tooth.") but not soft or sticky. When you cook pasta too long, it absorbs too much cooking liquid. As a result, when sauce is added, the dish can become weepy or watery. Pasta that is still a little firm is more likely to absorb some of the liquid from the sauce, thus preventing a soggy finished dish.

When the pasta is done, test it by cutting a piece with a fork, or taking a bite. The pasta will have only a slight bit of uncooked core, when it is al dente. Drain the cooked pasta at once, pouring it into a large strainer. A large pasta pot with a colander insert allows you to lift the pasta out of the boiling water at just the proper moment. Place drained pasta in a hot bowl and add the sauce. Serve at once.

If you are going to hold the pasta before serving (not recommended, but sometimes unavoidable) you should rinse it. Use lukewarm water and toss the pasta with a little olive oil to keep the strands separated.

CHOOSING THE RIGHT PASTA FOR YOUR SAUCE

You can combine any shape pasta with any sauce and the flavor will be just fine, but if you have a heavy sauce, especially one that has meat in it, you will probably find that a pasta that can

catch the sauce in its twists and curls, such as fusilli or small shells (conchiglie), will give you the most pleasing combination. Short, tubular pasta shapes, such as rigatoni and penne, are also good choices for heavy sauces.

A slippery oil-based sauce works well with long, thin pasta, such as cappellini (angel hair) or vermicelli. The oil will keep each strand separate. Tomato, cheese, and cream-based sauces combine well with the long, thick pasta shapes, such as linguine or spaghetti, and medium length tubular pastas, such as penne, rigatoni, and ziti. Experiment with the various pasta shapes and find your own favorite combinations.

Fresh versus Dried Pasta

Fresh pasta is almost always better than dried pasta. There are some excellent dried pastas available, but with fresh pasta, you enjoy the best "tooth' or consistency after cooking.

When you must choose a dried pasta, look for one made of durum wheat flour if it is a domestic brand. If the pasta is an Italian import, it should contain pure semolina flour.

About Tomatoes

Canned vs. Fresh Tomatoes

Tomatoes are the basis of some great sauces. The taste of a fresh tomato is so special that combined with a few herbs and scarcely cooked it can become the perfect complement for a light meal of linguine. Or it can be simmered with meat and wine and slowly cooked for hours to become a hearty soul-satisfying sauce for spaghetti.

If you can't get fresh, vine-ripened tomatoes for your sauces, use canned tomatoes. These tomatoes are ripened before they are canned, so the flavor is rich and intense. Canned tomatoes, already peeled and seeded, can't be beaten for convenience, either.

Peeling and Seeding Tomatoes

If you have fresh tomatoes, you will want them peeled and seeded for some recipes. This is easy to do. Just plunge the whole tomato in boiling water for 15 to 30 seconds. Remove to a bowl of ice water or run under cold tap water. The skin can then be easily peeled away with a paring knife. To seed a tomato, cut it in half and gently squeeze out the seeds. You can use a teaspoon to help finish the job.

Sun-Dried Tomatoes

The flavor of sun-dried tomatoes is richly intense. During the drying process, the natural sweetness and flavor of the ripe tomatoes are intensified. Tomatoes are usually packed with herbs and olive oil, resulting in ready-to-use tomatoes. Two tablespoons of chopped sun-dried tomatoes can transform a simple sauce into something really special. The oil that the tomatoes are packed in can be used in vegetable sautes and salad dressings. You can buy sun-dried tomatoes in specialty food stores and many better supermarkets. Be sure to buy the kind that are packed in oil.

If you grow your own tomatoes, it is well worth the effort to make your own dried tomatoes.

To dry tomatoes, select good ripe Italian plum tomatoes. Slice each tomato almost in half vertically and open like a book. Remove the stem end with a small V cut and cut off any blemishes. Place the open tomatoes skin side down on drying racks. Salt lightly.

To dry in a food dehydrator, set on high heat and dry for 10 to 16 hours, until the tomato halves are leathery but not dry or hard. Small tomatoes will dry faster than large ones. Check the dehydrator frequently and remove individual tomatoes as they dry.

When the tomatoes are dry, fold the tomato halves closed. Pack very tightly in halfpint jars, with sprigs of fresh herbs or slivers of garlic between the tomatoes. Pack the tomatoes upright and make 2 layers of tomatoes with herbs in each

layer. Fill with olive oil to completely cover everything.

Poke a fork around the edge of the jar to release any air bubbles. Seal the jars tightly. Store them at room temperature, or use immediately.

ABOUT CHEESE

Freshly grated Parmesan cheese is an ingredient in many sauces, and it is often served at the table for sprinkling over pasta. In Italy, Parmesan cheese is still produced in small factories from local cow milk by a method that has remained unchanged for centuries. The finished cheese, generally aged for over a year, is hard, straw colored, slightly crumbly, mellow, and salty.

A similar cheese, made from sheep's milk and aged for about 8 months, is Pecorino Romano. The flavor of Pecorino is somewhat more robust than that of Parmesan. You can substitute Parmesan for Pecorino Romano, but it is probably not a good idea to substitute Pecorino for Parmesan.

Don't buy grated cheese; it won't have the same rich flavor. Wrapped in foil, the hard cheese keeps well in the refrigerator for several months. Freshly grated cheese can be stored in an airtight container in the freezer for up to 6 weeks without any loss of flavor. A food processor fitted with a steel blade does a good job of grating the cheese. Many people enjoy the act of using hand graters or other available devices. The key is to grate only as needed for the best, richest flavor.

Chapter 1

Classic
Sauces

Tomato Meat Sauce

*Cook this thick, hearty sauce until the meat falls apart
and serve over a short pasta such as penne.*

**3/4 pound each lean sirloin steak
and pork tenderloin, well-trimmed
2 tablespoons olive oil
1/2 cup minced onion
3 garlic cloves, minced
1 medium-size carrot, minced
1 celery stalk, minced
1 cup chopped mushrooms
1 (6 ounce) can tomato paste
2 cups dry red wine
1 bay leaf
1/4 cup chopped fresh parsley
freshly ground black pepper to taste**

In a large skillet, brown the steak and pork over
medium-high heat about 10 minutes. Transfer the
meat to a plate and spoon fat from the skillet. Add
1/2 cup water to the skillet and bring to a boil,
scraping up any browned bits from the bottom. Set
the drippings aside. Heat olive oil in a large
saucepan. Add the onion, carrot, mushrooms and
celery. Sauté until tender, about 3 to 5 minutes.
Add the garlic and cook 1 minute longer. Add
tomato paste, reserved drippings, wine, bay leaf,
parsley and pepper. Add the meats and juices
from the plate. Simmer on very low heat, covered,
about 4 hours, or until the meats fall apart. Serves 4.

Bolognese Sauce

As the most well-known of Italian meat sauces, Bolognese Sauce improves with age, so if you have the time, make it a day ahead. It is a rich sauce, containing meat, onions, carrots, and butter traditionally made with veal and pork. We have adapted this classic to use ground sirloin and lean pork. It is the traditional sauce for lasagne and can be used over any kind of pasta.

2 tablespoons each olive oil and butter
1/2 cup chopped onion
1/2 cup chopped carrot
1/2 cup chopped green bell pepper OR
celery with some leaves
2 garlic cloves, minced
1/2 cup white wine
1/2 cup half-and-half
1 (28-ounce) can peeled Italian tomatoes, chopped
1 (15 ounce) can tomato sauce
1 tablespoon chopped fresh,
OR 1 teaspoon dried basil leaves,
1/2 teaspoon dried oregano
1 bay leaf
1/2 pound lean ground pork
1/2 pound ground sirloin
1 teaspoon salt, or to taste
1/4 teaspoon coarsely ground black pepper
1/2-inch by l-inch strip lemon peel (no white pith)

In a large pot, sauté onion, carrots, and green pep-

per or celery in oil and butter over low heat. Stir often, until vegetables are tender but not browned. Add garlic, basil, oregano, and bay leaf. Sauté 2 more minutes. Add salt and pepper to taste.

Lightly brown pork and beef in a skillet over medium-low heat. Skim excess fat and add the meat to the pot along with drippings from the pan. Add the wine. Raise the heat to medium high and cook, stirring often, until the wine evaporates, 8 to 10 minutes. Add the half and half. Reduce the heat and cook gently, stirring frequently, until the half and half has almost entirely reduced. Then add the tomatoes, tomato sauce and the lemon peel.

Cover and simmer gently, stirring occasionally, until the sauce has thickened, about 2 hours. Or bake in a 325° F. oven in a covered earthenware casserole until the sauce thickens, 1-1/2 to 2 hours. Remove the lemon peel before serving. Serves 4.

Roman Ragu

This hearty sauce with its blend of vegetables and meat could almost be called a stew.

3 to 4 tablespoons olive oil
1 large onion, chopped
1 celery stalk with leaves, thinly sliced
1 carrot, thinly sliced
1 cup fresh mushrooms, sliced
6 cloves garlic, minced, or more to taste
2 pounds lean ground beef
1 pound Italian sausage, casings removed
2 (28-ounce) cans Italian plum tomatoes, crushed
1 (6-ounce) can tomato paste
2 cups water
1 cup dry red wine
2 tablespoons chopped parsley
1/4 cup fresh basil, chopped
1 teaspoon dried oregano
1 bay leaf
salt and pepper to taste

Sauté onion, celery, carrot and mushrooms in the olive oil. Cook until vegetables are soft. Add the garlic and cook 1 or 2 minutes longer. Put the vegetables in a large pot. In same sauté pan, brown the meat. Skim off the fat then add to the vegetables along with the crushed tomatoes, tomato paste, water and wine. Stir to blend. Add remaining ingredients and simmer uncovered until thickened. About 1-1/2 hours. Serves 4 to 6.

Meaty Mushroom Sauce

1 pound ground sirloin
1 pound fresh mushrooms, sliced
2 tablespoons chopped onion
1 garlic clove, pressed
1 (15-ounce) can tomato sauce
1 (10-1/2-ounce) can tomato pureé
1 cup water
2 beef bouillon cubes
1 tablespoon grated fresh Parmesan cheese
1 teaspoon dried oregano
1 teaspoon sugar
1/2 teaspoon dried basil
1/8 teaspoon black pepper
1 cup tomato juice (optional)

In a large skillet, brown meat, mushrooms, onion and garlic. Add tomato sauce, tomato pureé, water, bouillon cubes, Parmesan cheese, oregano, sugar, basil and pepper. Stir to blend ingredients. Bring to a boil, cover and reduce heat, simmering for 30 minutes. Add 1/2 to 1 cup tomato juice for a thinner sauce. Serve over your favorite fresh pasta.

Marinara Sauce

This quick easy-to-make sauce, traditionally used by fishermen, can be varied by the addition of shellfish. Often served over angel hair pasta, it is an elegant solution for those with no time to fuss over their food.

4 cloves garlic, chopped
4 tablespoons olive oil
4 pounds fresh tomatoes OR
4 (14-1/2 ounce) cans plum tomatoes
1 teaspoon dried oregano
6 tablespoons of fresh parsley
salt and freshly ground black pepper to taste

Sauté garlic in olive oil. If using fresh tomatoes, remove skin by blanching in water for 30 seconds. Then cut off stem end and squeeze out seeds. If using canned tomatoes, drain the liquid. Chop tomatoes and add to pan with garlic along with remaining ingredients. Bring to a boil and simmer uncovered for about 20 minutes. Serves 4.

Alfredo Sauce

You can prepare this restaurant favorite in less than 10 minutes. It is extremely rich so serve it in small portions. Fettuccini is the traditional combination, but this sauce also complements broad pastas like farfalle (butterflies) or stuffed varieties such as tortellini. Adding fresh cooked peas and strips of prosciutto, ham or bacon is a common variation.

12 tablespoons butter
2 cups freshly grated Parmesan cheese
1 cup heavy cream
1 cup milk
1/2 cup chopped fresh parsley(optional)
freshly ground black pepper to taste

Melt the butter in a saucepan. Stir in the cheese. Then add the cream and milk and heat through. Be careful not to boil. Just before serving add pepper and parsley if desired. Serves 4.

LOWER-FAT VARIATION
2 cups skim milk
2 tablespoons imitation butter granules
12 wedges low-fat processed cheese, like Laughing Cow®
2 tablespoons freshly grated Parmesan cheese
Pinch of garlic powder

In a medium-sized saucepan or double boiler, combine all the ingredients until all is melted and the sauce is velvety smooth, about 20 minutes. Serves 4.

Bechamel Sauce

Baked dishes such as lasagne often include this white sauce, but bechamel also serves as a basic ingredient in many other sauce recipes. Season with garlic and herbs and add a cup of cooked shellfish or fish for a creamy white seafood sauce.

1-1/4 cups milk
1/2 bay leaf
1/4 cup butter
1/4 cup all-purpose flour
salt and white pepper to taste

In a small saucepan, heat milk and bay leaf over low heat to just below boiling point. Remove from heat. Remove and discard bay leaf. In a small saucepan, melt butter over medium heat. Stir in flour, cook 2 minutes, stirring constantly. Remove from heat. Gradually stir in hot milk. Return pan to heat. Stir until thick and smooth. Reduce heat to low and cook 10 minutes stirring occasionally. Season with salt and pepper. If sauce is not used immediately, cover surface tightly with plastic wrap.

HAM & MUSHROOM SAUCE VARIATION

2-1/2 cups sliced fresh mushrooms
3 tablespoons dry apple cider
1 cup shredded ham

24

grated nutmeg
***Bechamel Sauce made with 1-3/4 cups milk and
3 tablespoons each butter and all-purpose flour***

In a small saucepan, combine mushrooms with cider. Cover pan. Cook over low heat for about 5 minutes. Add mushrooms, cooking liquid, ham and nutmeg to the Bechamel Sauce. Toss with fettuccini or farfalle.

Sauce alla Puttanesca

Very loosely translated, Sauce alla Puttanesca means in the style of a prostitute. According to one of the many legends, the ladies would attract their clients with the enticing aroma of this flavorful and gutsy dish. Another story was that its quick preparation made it popular as a fast snack between clients.

3 tablespoons olive oil
2 garlic cloves, minced
4 cups peeled, chopped fresh Italian plum tomatoes or 1 (28-ounce) can Italian plum tomatoes, coarsely chopped (reserve and use the juice)
1/2 cup chopped, pitted, salt-cured black olives
2 teaspoons small capers, rinsed
1 teaspoon crushed red pepper, or to taste
1/2 teaspoon dried oregano
1 (2 ounce) can flat anchovies, drained, blotted dry, cut into small pieces
freshly ground black pepper to taste
2 tablespoons chopped Italian flat-leaf parsley

Heat oil in a large skillet add the garlic and sauté over low heat for about 1 minute; do not brown. Stir in tomatoes and their juice, olives, capers, red pepper, oregano and pepper. Cook over medium heat, stirring to break up tomatoes until the sauce thickens, about 15 minutes. Stir in anchovies and parsley. Simmer for 2 minutes and add salt to taste. Serves 4 to 6.

Chicken Liver and Sage Sauce

A Venetian classic that goes well over large tubular pasta like rigatoni, penne, or ziti.

2 tablespoons olive oil
1 pound chicken livers, trimmed and patted dry
1/2 cup chopped onion
3 garlic cloves, crushed
1/2 cup dry red wine
1 (28 ounce) can Italian plum tomatoes,
chopped with juices reserved
1/2 teaspoon crumbled dried sage
1/4 cup chopped Italian flat-leaf parsley
freshly grated Parmesan cheese
salt and freshly ground black pepper to taste

Heat oil in a large heavy skillet; sprinkle chicken livers with salt and pepper. Sauté in hot oil, turning often until the outsides are browned but they are still pink in the center, about 3 minutes. Transfer livers to a side dish. Add the onion to the skillet and simmer in the juices until tender, about 5 minutes. Add the garlic; cook 1 minute. Add wine and boil until reduced by half, about 5 minutes. Coarsely cut up the tomatoes while still in the can. Add tomatoes and sage to the skillet; heat to boiling. Cook sauce, stirring, over medium heat 10 minutes, or until slightly thickened. Coarsely chop the chicken livers; transfer livers and their juices to the sauce. Simmer briefly; stir in parsley. Season with salt and pepper. Pass with grated Parmesan cheese. Serves 6.

White Garlic Sauce

Popular lore prescribes garlic to ward off vampires and other evil spirits. Ancient Greeks thought it gave strength to harvesters. Modern-day herbalists regard garlic as a blood cleanser and recommend it for the prevention and treatment of the common cold. You can do nothing tastier to your homemade pasta than toss it with this delicate blend of garlic and olive oil. Clams or mussels make a great addition.

3/4 cup olive oil
4 cloves garlic, minced

Sauté the garlic in the oil over low heat until it just starts to brown. Do not overcook the garlic or the sauce will be bitter. Toss the garlic and oil with hot pasta and garnish with fresh chopped parsley and Parmesan cheese.

VARIATIONS

For a change, add one teaspoon of crushed red chili pepper while cooking, or use oil-cured black olives for the garnish. Add black pepper or oregano for extra seasoning.

Steam 2 dozen clams or mussels in white wine or water and add them to the oil in or out of their shells. You can substitute a 10-ounce can(drained) of whole or minced clams for fresh ones.

White Clam Sauce

Fresh shucked clams can be bought at your local fish market, but canned clams can be substituted. Serve this classic sauce over angel hair, vermicelli or spaghetti.

1/4 cup olive oil
2 tablespoons butter
2 garlic cloves, minced
1/4 cup chopped shallots
1 cup bottled clam juice
1/2 cup white wine
2 cups fresh minced clams
1/2 cup chopped fresh parsley

In a saucepan, heat the olive oil and butter over medium heat. Add the garlic and shallots and sauté until they just start to brown, 4 to 5 minutes. Add the clam juice and wine and simmer for 5 minutes. Stir in the clams and parsley. Bring the sauce to a boil, then remove from the heat. Pass with freshly grated Parmesan cheese. Serves 4.

Anchovy Sauce

This wonderfully simple, but satisfying dish allows the flavor of the anchovies to delicately combine with the butter, olive oil and garlic.

1/4 cup butter
1/4 cup olive oil
4 garlic cloves, minced
2 anchovies, minced
1/3 cup dry white wine
1/4 cup finely chopped Italian flat-leaf parsley
freshly ground black pepper to taste

Heat the butter and oil in a saucepan over medium heat. Add the garlic and sauté until golden, about 3 minutes. Blend in the anchovies and wine and cook over low heat. Stir constantly, until the anchovies have dissolved into the sauce, about 10 minutes. Stir in the parsley and black pepper. Serves 4.

Sauce con Sarde

The Mediterranean Sea is a bountiful resource for fishermen. This pasta sauce with sardines is a classic dish from Sicily.

6 tablespoons olive oil
1/2 cup chopped onions
3 flat anchovy fillets, drained, blotted dry
and finely chopped
1/4 cup finely chopped feathery leaves
from fresh fennel
1/4 cup pine nuts
1 tablespoon raisins, soaked in boiling water
for 10 minutes, drained
1(3-3/4 ounce) can sardines packed in oil,
drained and patted dry
toasted bread crumbs

Heat the oil in a large skillet. Add onion and sauté until golden about 5 minutes. Add anchovies and sauté over low heat stirring constantly until they are dissolved. Add the fennel, pine nuts, raisins and sardines. Heat through, stirring gently for about minutes more. Garnish with bread crumbs. Serves 4.

Carbonara Sauce

This is a typically Roman dish that uses Pecorino Romano, a goat's milk cheese, and pancetta, a cured but not smoked bacon. It was first popularized by allied soldiers during World War II. The word carbonara comes from carbon, meaning "coal," so it has been suggested that the name originated because the mixing bowl was so heavily coated with black pepper that it looked like a coal cellar.

4 tablespoons butter
1-1/2 teaspoons coarsely ground black pepper
1/4 pound pancetta or Canadian bacon, cut in slivers
4 eggs
3 tablespoons half and half
salt to taste
1 cup grated Pecorino Romano or Parmesan cheese
1 tablespoon chopped fresh chives

Melt 2 tablespoons butter in a skillet, add the pancetta, and sauté for about 2 minutes. Meanwhile, generously grease a large serving bowl with butter and coat it with the black pepper and set it aside. Remove pancetta from the heat and keep warm. In a medium-size bowl, beat the eggs with the half and half and salt. Add to the pancetta and cook over medium heat, stirring, until eggs begin to thicken slightly. Stir in chives. Slowly add the egg mixture to hot pasta, tossing continuously. Pour immediately into the pepper-coated serving bowl. Add cheese, and mix well. Serves 4.

Classic Basil Pesto

This classic basil paste compliments a wide variety of pasta dishes, including cold pasta salads. The name derives from the word pestle, as the original pesto was made in a mortar and pestle. Just remember never to heat pesto before putting it on pasta, or it will separate.

**2 cups lightly packed fresh basil leaves
4 garlic cloves, minced
1/4 cup pine nuts or walnuts
1/2 cup freshly grated Parmesan cheese
2 tablespoons freshly grated
Pecorino Romano cheese
1/2 cup olive oil
salt and freshly ground pepper to taste**

Wash, pat dry, and stem the basil leaves. Put basil, garlic, pine nuts and salt in a mortar, blender or food processor. Pulverize until you have a smooth paste. Add the cheese and mix until thoroughly combined. Slowly blend in the olive oil. Salt and pepper to taste. Let stand for 5 minutes.

When basil is out of season, try parsley instead. Thin the pesto with a few tablespoons of cream or hot pasta cooking water before tossing with hot pasta. Makes about 1 cup and serves 4.

Pasta Primavera

There are many different vegetable combinations you can use for pasta primavera. Fresh seasonal vegetables will yield the tastiest results. Usually no more than three different vegetables are used in combination, as in this spring-vegetable combination of peas, asparagus, and red pepper. Other tasty combinations include zucchini, mushrooms, and string beans; broccoli, red pepper, and snow peas; peas, yellow squash, and cherry tomatoes; and broccoli, cauliflower, and red pepper. A total of 6 to 7 cups of fresh vegetables will feed 4 generously.

**2 cups fresh shelled peas
(approximately 1-1/2 pounds peas in pod)
10 fresh asparagus spears, cut in 1-1/2 inch lengths
2 cups sweet red pepper in 2-inch strips
1/2 cup butter
1-1/4 cups all-purpose cream
1/2 cup freshly grated Parmesan cheese
2 tablespoons olive oil
1/3 cup pine nuts
1 garlic clove, chopped
1/4 cup chopped fresh Italian parsley
salt and freshly ground pepper to taste**

Blanch each vegetable separately in boiling salted water for 2 to 3 minutes, until just barely tender. Drain and rinse under cold running water to halt the cooking process. This step can be done 4 to 6 hours before you are ready to serve. Store the blanched vegetables in a covered container in the

refrigerator. (Note: If you are substituting cherry tomatoes or mushrooms for the vegetables above, do not blanch. Instead, saute in a little olive oil with a minced garlic clove. Cook tomatoes until soft; they should still retain their shape. Cooking mushrooms for about 3 minutes.)Melt the butter in a large saucepan. Stir in the cream and Parmesan cheese. Cook over low heat until the cheese is melted. Keep warm. Heat the olive oil in a large skillet. Add the pine nuts and cook over medium-low heat until pale gold. Add the garlic, blanched vegetables,and parsley. Stir gently until the vegetables are heated through, 3 to 5 minutes. Remove from the heat and keep warm in a large bowl. To serve, pour the warm cream sauce over hot pasta (spaghetti or fusilli is recommended) and toss thoroughly. (If the sauce is too thick, thin with additional cream.) Add one-third of the vegetables to the pasta and toss again. Season with salt and pepper. Divide the pasta among 4 heated plates and spoon the remaining vegetables over each serving. Serve immediately. Serves 4.

Sauce All' Amatriciana

This pasta sauce is said to have originated in the town of Amatrice, north of Rome. It is a simple tomato and lean bacon mixture usually served over thick spaghetti and topped with Pecorino cheese. The pasta in this classic is a thin hollow tube in the shape of a drinking straw. You may find it labeled bucatini, perciatelli, or in a thinner version perciatellini.

6 tablespoons olive oil
1/2 cup chopped onion
8 strips lightly smoked, lean bacon
1 (28 ounce) can whole peeled tomatoes, drained
pinch of crushed dried red pepper
salt to taste
freshly grated Pecorino Romano cheese

Heat oil in a large skillet. Add onion and sauté over low heat, stirring until golden. Add bacon and sauté 2 more minutes. Squeeze juice and seeds from tomatoes and chop. Add tomatoes to skillet and cook, stirring, over medium heat, until softened and sauce is slightly thickened about another 15 minutes. Add red pepper and salt to taste. Pass with grated Pecorino Romano cheese. Serves 4.

Chapter 2

Cream
Sauces

Four Cheeses Sauce

A sophisticated macaroni and cheese, this creamy blend of four cheeses is traditionally mixed with bucatini, a thin hollow tube pasta.

**1-1/4 cups half and half
1/2 cup grated Parmesan cheese (1-1/2 ounces)
3 ounces Gruyere cheese, diced
3 ounces soft goat's cheese
3 ounces mozzarella cheese, diced
freshly ground black pepper to taste
chopped ham, optional
chopped chives, optional**

Put half and half in a large saucepan with half of Parmesan cheese. Add Gruyere cheese, goat's cheese and mozzarella cheese. Cook over low heat until cheeses are melted. Season with pepper to taste. Add cooked and drained bucatini or macaroni to cheese mixture. Stir well. Sprinkle with remaining Parmesan cheese, ham and chives, if desired. Serves 4.

Creamy Mushroom & Pea Sauce

1/3 cup butter
2 cups sliced mushrooms
2/3 cup creme fraîche
2 egg yolks
1/2 cup grated Parmesan cheese
salt and freshly ground black pepper to taste
and nutmeg to taste
1-1/2 cups frozen green peas
fresh mint, optional

In a medium-size skillet, melt 2 tablespoons of butter. Add mushrooms. Sauté gently until tender. Set aside. In a medium-size bowl, beat together creme fraîche, egg yolks, parmesan cheese, salt, pepper and nutmeg. In a medium-size saucepan, melt remaining butter. Stir in creme fraîche mixture. Add peas. Cook over very low heat, stirring, until mixture is heated through and begins to thicken slightly. Stir in cooked mushrooms. Serve over hot pasta at once and garnish with mint, if desired. Serves 4.

Green & Blue Sauce

1/2 pound fresh broccoli
6 ounces Gorgonzola cheese
1/2 cup mascarpone
1 cup plain yogurt
freshly ground black pepper to taste

Wash and trim broccoli, discarding stalks. Cut in small florettes. Cook in boiling salted water 2 to 3 minutes or until crisp-tender. Drain thoroughly. Roughly chop cheese. Put cheese and mascarpone in a small saucepan. Stir over low heat until cheese has melted. Add broccoli and yogurt to cheese sauce. Heat gently, stirring occasionally, 2 minutes. Pour over hot pasta. Serves 4.

Artichoke Hearts and Cream

Be sure to use artichoke hearts packed in water. They are far superior to frozen artichoke hearts, which are usually mushy. Each can contains 5 to 7 hearts. This sauce goes well over spaghetti or linguine.

10 bacon slices
2 tablespoons butter
1/2 cup sliced scallions, including the green tops
1/2 cup whipping cream OR half-and-half
1/2 cup freshly grated Parmesan cheese
1/4 cup minced fresh parsley
salt and freshly ground black pepper to taste
2 (14-ounce) cans artichoke hearts packed
in water, drained and halved
freshly grated Parmesan cheese for topping

Fry the bacon until crisp. Drain on paper towels; set aside. When cool, crumble. In a large skillet, melt the butter over medium heat. Add the scallions and sauté for 3 minutes. Add the cream and simmer until the sauce thickens slightly. Add Parmesan cheese and the parsley. Season with salt and pepper to taste. Add the artichokes and heat through. Serve over hot pasta. Top with the crumbled bacon and pass with additional Parmesan cheese. Serves 4 to 6.

Ricotta, Leek & Ham Sauce

2 tablespoons butter
2 leeks, thinly sliced
1 garlic clove, crushed
1 ounce thin ham slices
2 cups ricotta cheese
2/3 cup dairy sour cream
milk
freshly ground black pepper to taste

In a medium-size saucepan over medium heat, melt butter; add leeks and garlic. Cook until leeks are soft. Cut ham into small squares. Stir into leeks. Cook a few minutes more.

In a medium-size bowl, mix together ricotta and sour cream. Add a little milk, if necessary, to make a smooth creamy sauce. Season with pepper. Add to pan with leeks and ham. Reduce heat to low and cook until sauce is heated through. Serve at once over hot pasta. Serves 4.

Tomato Cream Sauce

There's always another way to enjoy pasta. This combination is rich and smooth.

1 cup heavy cream
1/2 stick butter
3 ounces soft processed Gruyere cheese
1 cup warmed marinara sauce (See recipe page 22)

In a medium-sized saucepan or double boiler, combine the heavy cream, butter, and cheese. Cook over a low heat until everything is melted and the sauce is velvety smooth, about 20 minutes. Add the warmed marinara sauce, mix together. For some added crunch, add a 16-ounce bag of frozen cauliflower, broccoli, and carrot combination that has been thawed and blanched Toss with hot pasta. Serves 4.

Walnut Sauce

This creamy nut sauce has a unique texture and flavor.

**8 ounces shelled walnuts
4 tablespoons breadcrumbs
2 cloves garlic
4 tablespoons olive oil
3/4 cup milk**

Blanch the walnuts in boiling water and rub off their skins. Soak the breadcrumbs in water, then drain and squeeze dry. Place the walnuts, breadcrumbs, and garlic in a blender or food processor and blend until a smooth paste forms. Add the olive oil, milk, and salt to taste and stir well. Toss cooked pasta with sauce. Serves 4.

Green Peppercorn & Lemon Sauce

This delicate sauce is ideal for serving with angel hair or other fine pasta.

2 tablespoons butter
2/3 cup half and half
1 to 2 teaspoons green peppercorns, drained
grated peel of 1 lemon
salt to taste

In a small saucepan, melt butter. Stir in half and half. Lightly crush peppercorns with the back of a spoon. Add to sauce. Stir in lemon peel and salt to taste. Cook over low heat, without boiling, until slightly thickened. Toss with hot pasta. Serves 4.

Wine & Cream Sauce

This mellow sauce is perfect in combination with a variety of seafood or poultry additions. Use your creativity.

**1/4 cup butter
1 small onion, finely chopped
1 bay leaf
2 parsley sprigs with long stalks
1/2 cup button mushrooms, thinly sliced
1/3 cup all-purpose flour
1-1/2 cups dry white wine
3/4 cup stock (chicken, vegetable
or fish, depending on the dish)
salt
freshly ground white or black pepper to taste
1-1/2 cups light cream**

Melt the butter in a saucepan. Add the onion, bay leaf and parsley, and cook, stirring often, for 15 minutes, or until the onion is softened slightly but not browned. Stir in the mushrooms, then stir in the flour. Gradually stir in the white wine and stock. Beat well then stir in bay leaf and parsley. Bring to a boil. The sauce will be too thick at this stage. Cover the pan tightly and allow the sauce to cook very gently for 15 minutes. Remove the bay leaf and parsley sprigs. Stir in the cream and heat gently without boiling. Add your choice of seafood such as cooked whole shrimp or pieces of boneless cooked chicken breast and heat through. Toss with hot pasta. Serves 4.

Tomato-Dill Cream Sauce

Here's a way to take something simple and make it look and taste fancy with no fuss at all!

**1/2 cup mayonnaise
1 cup (1/2 pint) half-and-half
1/4 cup chopped fresh dill
2 medium-sized tomatoes, finely chopped
3 scallions, finely chopped
salt and freshly ground black pepper to taste**

In a saucepan, mix together the mayonnaise, half-and-half, and chopped dill; cook over medium heat, stirring occasionally, until the mixture is heated through. Remove from the stove; stir in the tomatoes, scallion, salt, and pepper. Serve immediately over hot pasta and sprinkle with grated Parmesan cheese, if desired. Serves 4.

Chapter 3

Red
Sauces

Tomato Wine Sauce

This simple sauce is great over flavored pastas such as spinach fettuccini or garlic and herb linguine.

**1 tablespoon olive oil
1 medium-sized onion, chopped
2 garlic cloves, minced
8 medium tomatoes, seeded and cubed
1 teaspoon sugar
1/2 teaspoon dried basil
1/3 cup red wine
3/4 cup beef broth
1 tablespoon wine vinegar
1 teaspoon salt
1 teaspoon pepper**

In a large skillet, sauté the onion and garlic in oil over a medium-high heat until the onion is tender. Add the remaining ingredients to the skillet, and stir. Reduce heat, and simmer for 15 to 20 minutes, or until the mixture is heated through. Be careful not to overcook. Toss with pasta and serve. Serves 4.

Tomato & Olive Sauce

This sauce is easy to make and goes well over just about any type pasta.

6 fresh medium tomatoes, diced
2 bunches fresh basil, shredded
1/2 cup chopped parsley
3 sun-dried tomatoes, chopped
2 tablespoons pine nuts, toasted
1/2 log Montrachet cheese, cut in small pieces
1/2 cup ripe olives, cut in half
salt and freshly ground black pepper to taste
1 tablespoon Herbs de Provence
1/2 cup olive oil
1/2 cup red wine vinegar
1/4 teaspoon sugar
1/2 teaspoon Dijon-style mustard
3 garlic cloves, minced

Combine fresh tomatoes, basil, parsley, sun-dried tomatoes, pine nuts, Montrachet, olives, salt, pepper and Herbs de Provence in a large bowl and set aside. In a small bowl or blender, combine the oil, vinegar, sugar, mustard and garlic; blend well and set aside. Toss tomato and oil mixtures with hot pasta in a large heated bowl. Serves 4.

Garden Lamb Sauce

This sauce, perfect for a late August supper, is especially good tossed with penne, ziti, or fusilli.

5 tablespoons olive oil
1 cup chopped Spanish onion
1 medium red bell pepper, stems and
seeds removed, diced
1 medium green bell pepper, stems and
seeds removed, diced
1 eggplant, peeled, and cut into 1/2-inch cubes
1 pound fresh ripe tomatoes, cored and diced
3 tablespoons of tomato paste
1/2 cup dry red wine
1 clove garlic, crushed
1 teaspoon salt
salt and freshly ground black pepper to taste
2 tablespoons chopped fresh basil
3/4 cup lean ground lamb, pork or beef
freshly grated Parmesan cheese

Heat olive oil in a large skillet. Add onion and red and green peppers; sauté until tender, about 10 minutes. Add eggplant; cook over high heat stirring frequently until eggplant begins to brown about 5 minutes. Stir in tomatoes, tomato paste, wine, garlic, salt, pepper and basil. Cook, stirring, 5 minutes. Meanwhile, in a deep saucepan, sauté meat over medium high heat. Drain fat and add tomato/eggplant mixture. Simmer for 30 minutes. Toss with hot pasta. Serves 4.

Sausage and Peppers Sauce

This meaty sauce pleases hearty appetites and works well with penne or spaghetti.

1/2 pound Italian-style sausage
3 tablespoons olive oil
2 green bell peppers, seeded, cut into 1/2-inch strips
1 small onion, cut into 1/2-inch chunks
1 garlic clove, crushed
1 (28 ounce) can Italian plum tomatoes,
drained and chopped
1/4 teaspoon oregano
salt and freshly ground black pepper to taste

Cut the sausage into 1/2-inch crosswise slices. Sauté in a medium skillet over low heat, stirring, until browned, about 10 minutes. Lift from pan with a slotted spoon; discard any sausage drippings and wipe out the pan. Heat the oil in the skillet; sauté the peppers and onion over medium heat, stirring until edges begin to brown and vegetables are crisp-tender, about 5 minutes. Then add the garlic and sauté for 1 minute. Return the sausage to the skillet and add tomatoes, oregano, salt and pepper. Cook, stirring, uncovered, for 5 minutes to concentrate the tomato juices. Add the seasonings and simmer for 5 more minutes. Toss with hot pasta. Serves 4.

Beef in Wine Tomato Sauce

Boneless beef roast simmers to moist tenderness in a spicy tomato sauce. Top with fresh mint.

2 tablespoons olive oil
1 large onion, finely chopped
4 cloves garlic, slivered
1 boneless beef chuck roast (3 to 3-1/2 lbs.),
trimmed of fat and cut into 1-inch cubes
1 cup each dry red wine and water
1 (8 ounce) can tomato sauce
2 tablespoons red wine vinegar
1 dry bay leaf
5 whole allspice
1 cinnamon stick (about 3 inches long)
1 teaspoon cumin seeds
1/2 teaspoon each salt and pepper
2 to 3 tablespoons chopped fresh mint leaves

Heat oil in a large frying pan over medium-high heat. Add onion, garlic and meat and cook, stirring often, until onion is soft and meat is evenly brown (8 to 10 minutes). Transfer meat to a large Dutch oven. Stir in wine, water, tomato sauce, vinegar, bay leaf, allspice, cinnamon stick, cumin seeds, salt, and pepper. Bring to a boil, then cover and cook on very low heat until meat is very tender when pierced (1-1/2 to 2 hours). Skim and discard fat; remove and discard bay leaf and cinnamon. Serve over hot pasta and garnish with mint. Serves 6 to 8.

Sweet-Sour Chicken Sauce

Distinctively seasoned with allspice, currants, and pine nuts, this fresh tomato sauce is delightful with tender linguine and strips of grilled chicken.

5 tablespoons olive oil
1 medium-size onion, thinly sliced
2 tablespoons pine nuts or slivered almonds
2 cloves garlic, minced or pressed
6 Roma tomatoes, chopped
1 tablespoon each firmly packed brown sugar
and dried currants
2 tablespoons cider vinegar
1/2 teaspoon ground allspice
3/4 cup dry red wine
2 whole chicken breasts (about 1 pound each),
skinned, boned, and split
salt and freshly ground black pepper to taste
chopped parsley

Heat 1/4 cup of the oil in a wide frying pan over medium heat. Add onion and pine nuts and cook, stirring, until onion is soft (about 5 minutes). Stir in garlic, tomatoes, sugar, currants, vinegar, allspice, and wine. Adjust heat so mixture boils gently. Continue to cook, uncovered, stirring occasionally, until sauce is slightly thickened (12 to 15 minutes).

Meanwhile, rinse chicken and pat dry. Brush on all sides with remaining 1 tablespoon oil. Place a ridged cooktop grill pan over medium heat; heat

56

until a drop of water dances on the surface. Place chicken on hot pan and cook, turning once, until well browned on outside and no longer pink in center; cut chicken in thickest part to test (about 10 minutes total). You can also grill chicken on an outdoor grill using a little garlic, olive oil, butter and lemon juice as a baste.

Season tomato sauce to taste with salt and pepper. Add hot pasta and gently toss. Transfer to a warm deep platter. Cut chicken into 1/2-inch-wide strips and arrange around edge of pasta. Garnish with parsley. Serves 4.

Sicilian Olive Sauce

A rich Mediterranean taste that's a meal in itself when served over spaghetti or linguini.

**2 cloves garlic, chopped
2 tablespoons olive oil
1 (28 ounce) can plum tomatoes, drained
1/2 teaspoon dried oregano
3 tablespoons of fresh parsley
1 (6 ounce) jar red roasted peppers,
drained and coarsely chopped
1 (6 ounce) jar marinated artichoke hearts
1 (6 ounce) can pitted ripe olives, drained
2 cooked boneless and skinless
chicken breasts, chunked
salt and freshly ground black pepper to taste**

Sauté garlic in olive oil. Chop tomatoes and add to pan with garlic along with remaining ingredients. Bring to a boil and simmer uncovered for about 20 minutes. Toss with hot pasta. Serves 4.

Chapter 4

Seafood Sauces

Tuna Carbonara

This colorful dish is a good choice for a spur-of-the-moment supper. The cooked pasta (uncoiled vermicelli is recommended) is coated with beaten egg, which helps the cheese, bell pepper strips and tuna cling to it.

2 tablespoons olive oil
2 tablespoons butter
1 large red bell pepper, seeded
and cut into thin bite-size strips
3 cloves garlic, minced or pressed
1 (9-1/4 ounce) can chunk-style tuna, drained
4 eggs, beaten until blended
1 cup freshly grated Parmesan cheese
1/4 cup chopped fresh parsley
salt and freshly ground black pepper to taste

Heat oil and butter in a wide frying pan over medium-high heat. Add bell pepper and garlic; cook, stirring often, until pepper is soft about 6 to 8 minutes. Meanwhile, cook and drain pasta.

Add cooked pasta and tuna to frying pan. Mix lightly, using 2 forks, just until mixture is heated through. Remove from heat. Then add eggs, cheese, and parsley. Mix lightly, lifting with 2 forks, until pasta is well coated with sauce. Season to taste with salt and pepper. Serves 4.

Calamari Sauce

Calamari, or squid, is becoming increasingly available and inexpensive. Cook the squid for this garlic-accented pasta main dish very briefly—just until the meat is opaque white. Overcooking can make the delicate shellfish unpleasantly tough. To clean the squid simply grasp the squid with one hand, reach inside the body and pull the head and tentacles away. Pull off and discard the mottled skin. Feel inside the body for the transparent cartilage (it looks and feels like plastic); draw it out and discard it. Then wash the body inside and out under cold running water. Separate the two flaps from the body; they pull away easily. Locate the ink sac, which is attached to the head, remove, and discard it. Then cut the tentacles from the head. Cut the body into thick rings, slice the flaps into strips and cut the tentacles to an easily forked size.

1 pound cleaned squid tubes (mantles) and tentacles
1/3 cup olive oil
1 large red onion, thinly sliced and
separated into rings
3 large cloves garlic, minced or pressed
1 tablespoon lemon juice
1/4 cup finely chopped parsley
lemon wedges
salt and freshly ground pepper to taste

Cut squid tubes crosswise into 1/2-inch-wide strips; set squid strips and tentacles aside. Heat oil in a wide frying pan over medium heat. Add onion and

cook, stirring often, until very soft but not brown (8 to 10 minutes).

To onion, add garlic and squid strips and tentacles; cook, stirring constantly, just until squid is opaque (2 to 3 minutes). Mix in lemon juice. Add hot pasta and half the parsley; mix gently, using 2 spoons, until heated through. Season to taste with salt and pepper. Sprinkle with remaining parsley and garnish with lemon wedges. Serves 4.

Smoked Salmon Sauce

3 tablespoons butter
1/4 cup chopped shallots
3 scallions, including some green tops, thinly sliced
1 cup finely chopped mushrooms
1 cup dry vermouth or dry white wine
1-1/2 cups half-and-half
2 tablespoons flour
1 pound smoked salmon, cut into bite-size pieces
2 tablespoons chopped fresh dill
salt and freshly ground black pepper to taste

Melt the butter in a medium-size skillet over medium heat. Add the shallots, scallions, and mushrooms and saute for 3 minutes. Add 3/4 cup of the vermouth or wine. Reduce the heat and slowly cook until the liquid has reduced by half. Add the half-and-half and increase the heat to medium, stirring the sauce until it is hot but not bubbling.

Make a thin paste by combining the flour with the remaining 1/4 cup vermouth or wine. Slowly add to the sauce, stirring constantly, and cook until the sauce has thickened, 3 to 5 minutes. Add the salmon, dill, and salt and pepper. Stir to blend and cook for 3 minutes. Serve over hot pasta. Serves 4.

Mussels with Curried Cream

4 pounds mussels in shell
3/4 cup dry white wine
4 tablespoons olive oil
1/2 teaspoon curry powder
1/2 cup chopped shallots
2 cups chopped mushrooms
1-1/2 cups chopped ripe tomatoes
3/4 to 1 cup light cream
1/4 cup minced fresh parsley

Scrub the mussels to remove any dirt. Pull off the beards (a twisted fiber connected to the shell). Discard any mussels that are open. In a large pot, combine the mussels with the wine and 2 tablespoons of the oil. Cover, bring to a boil, and steam the mussels over high heat for 5 minutes, or until the shells have opened. Discard any unopened mussels. Remove the mussels from the shells. Strain the liquid through a fine sieve. Reserve the broth.

In a medium-size saucepan, heat the remaining 2 tablespoons olive oil. Add curry, shallots and mushrooms. Sauté, stirring constantly, until the shallots and mushrooms soften slightly. Add some reserved mussel broth at intervals stirring and allowing to reduce. When all the broth has been added, and the amount of liquid has reduced to 1 to 1 1/2 cups, add the chopped tomatoes. Cook for 2 minutes, stirring constantly. Fold in the mussels and add cream to the desired consistency. Toss gently with hot pasta such as tomato spirals or tiny seashells. Serves 4.

Barbecued Crab Sauce

Served in a spicy barbecue sauce atop a platter of steaming spaghetti, crab is at its messiest and most delicious here. You eat the crab legs and claws with your fingers, so be sure to provide plenty of paper napkins.

2 tablespoons butter or margarine
1 large onion, finely chopped
3 cloves garlic, minced or pressed
1 (14-1/2ounce)can regular-strength chicken broth
1 (8 ounces) can tomato sauce
1 cup catsup
1/3 cup each white wine vinegar and
firmly packed brown sugar
3 tablespoons Worcestershire
1 tablespoon soy sauce
1-1/2 teaspoons dry mustard
1 teaspoon liquid hot pepper seasoning (Tabasco)
I/2 teaspoon each celery seeds, ground allspice,
and dry thyme leaves
2 bay leaves
2 large Dungeness crabs (3-1/2 to 4 pounds
total),cooked, cleaned, and cracked
chopped parsley

Melt butter in a 5 to 6 quart pan over medium-low heat. Add onion and garlic; cook, stirring often, until onion is soft but not brown (8 to 10 minutes). Stir in broth, tomato sauce, catsup, vinegar, sugar, Worcestershire, soy sauce, mustard, hot pepper sea-

soning, celery seeds, allspice, thyme, and bay leaves. Increase heat to high and bring to a boil; reduce heat and boil very gently, uncovered, until reduced to 3 cups (about 45 minutes).

Meanwhile, remove body meat from crabs, discarding shells. Set shelled body meat and cracked claws and legs aside. While pasta is cooking, add all shelled crab to sauce and simmer, uncovered, just until crab is heated through, stirring gently several times (about 5 minutes). Serve over hot pasta and sprinkle with parsley. Pass with cracked claws and legs on the side. Serves 4 to 6.

Salmon and Lemon Sauce

1/4 cup olive oil
1/2 cup vertically sliced onion
2 garlic cloves, crushed
1 teaspoon finely shredded lemon zest
2 tablespoons lemon juice
2 tablespoons coarsely chopped
Italian flat-leaf parsley
1 (7-3/4 ounce) can red salmon, drained
freshly grated Parmesan cheese

Heat oil in a skillet over low heat; stir in onion slices. Sauté, stirring, until tender but not browned, about 10 minutes. Add garlic. Sauté 2 minutes. Stir in lemon zest, juice, and parsley. Add salmon; carefully break up with a fork. Do not stir.

Reheat sauce over high heat; do not stir. Toss linguini and sauce together. Serve at once sprinkled with Parmesan. Serves 4.

Shellfish Sauce

1/3 cup olive oil
1 pound fresh mussels in shells, cleaned
1 garlic clove, crushed
2 shallots, finely chopped
1/2 pound medium-size peeled and deveined shrimp
2/3 cup dry white wine
salt and freshly ground black pepper to taste
1 (8-ounce) can clams, drained
2 tablespoons chopped fresh parsley

In a deep skillet with a cover, heat 3 tablespoons of olive oil. Add mussels. Cover pan; cook over medium heat about 4 minutes until all mussels are open. Discard mussels that do not open. Heat remaining oil in a medium-size saucepan. Add garlic, shallots and shrimp. Cook until shallots are soft and shrimp turns pink. Remove shrimp and set aside. Drain mussels. Strain cooking liquid. Add liquid and white wine to shallots and garlic. Bring to a boil. Boil gently, uncovered, until reduced slightly. Season with salt and pepper. Remove most mussels from shells, leaving a few for garnishing. Add mussels, shrimp and clams to cooking juice. Gently toss with hot pasta. Garnish with fresh parsley. Serves 4.

Mussels and Saffron Cream Sauce

Fresh mussels and fresh pasta are the key here. There are usually 18 medium-sized mussels to a pound so there will be plenty to go around. Fettuccine, tagliatelle, or linguine are recommended.

1 cup dry white wine
1 thickly sliced onion
1 strip orange zest (2 x 1/2 inch)
2 garlic cloves, bruised with side of a knife
8 saffron threads
2 pounds mussels, scrubbed and de-bearded
1 cup heavy cream
1 teaspoon fresh lemon juice

Combine the wine, onion, orange zest, garlic, and 4 of the saffron threads in a large wide saucepan; cover and heat to boiling. Add the mussels; cover and cook over high heat until mussels have opened, about 5 minutes. With tongs, transfer mussels to a bowl; cool slightly.

Meanwhile, boil the wine and mussel juice mixture left in the saucepan until reduced by about half, then pour through a very fine mesh sieve to remove any grit. Wipe out saucepan and return reduced wine mixture to saucepan. Stir in heavy cream and the remaining 4 saffron threads and boil gently until reduced by half and slightly thickened. Stir in the lemon juice. Toss sauce with hot pasta and top with mussels. Serves 4.

Ginger Smoked Scallop Sauce

The woodsy flavor of oven-smoked scallops blends hauntingly with fresh ginger and cream in this rich sauce that goes well over linguine or fettuccini.

**1 pound scallops, rinsed and patted dry
3 tablespoons liquid smoke
1-1/2 tablespoons each tarragon wine vinegar
and grated fresh ginger
1/4 cup thinly sliced shallots
1 cup whipping cream
1/2 cup dry white wine
1 teaspoon Dijon mustard
chopped fresh parsley**

If scallops are large, cut them into bite-size pieces. Pour liquid smoke into a 5 to 6 quart pan with ovenproof handles. Set a perforated or wire rack in pan. Arrange scallops in a single layer on rack and cover tightly. Bake in a 350° F. oven until scallops are opaque throughout about 12 to 15 minutes (cut to test).While scallops are smoking, cook pasta. While pasta is cooking, combine vinegar, ginger, and shallots in a wide frying pan over high heat. Cook until vinegar has evaporated (about 1 minute). Add cream, wine, and mustard. Bring to a full boil; then boil, uncovered, stirring often, until sauce is reduced to 1-1/4 cups. Reduce heat to medium; add scallops and mix lightly until heated through (1 to 2 minutes). Toss gently with hot pasta and sprinkle with parsley. Serves 4.

Shrimp & Garlic Butter Sauce

This version of the well-known favorite, Shrimp Scampi, is a simple sauce that doesn't overpower the succulent taste of shrimp. Serve with spaghetti or linguini.

2 tablespoons olive oil
1/3 cup butter
2 garlic cloves, finely chopped
1/2 pound shrimp, cooked, peeled, deveined
salt and freshly ground black pepper to taste
2 tablespoons chopped fresh chives

In a small saucepan, heat oil and butter over medium heat until butter is melted. Add garlic. Cook, stirring occasionally, 2 to 3 minutes. Stir in shrimp. Cook until heated through. Season with salt and pepper. Toss with hot pasta. Sprinkle with chives. Serves 4.

Chapter 5

Innovative
Sauces

Tri-Color Sauce

A rich, buttery sauce for people who don't count calories. Serve with rotini, ziti or farfelle (butterflies).

1/2 cup butter
1/2 cup fresh or frozen peas
1 large sweet yellow pepper, julienned
1-1/2 cups medium or light cream
1 pound fresh plum tomatoes, peeled and diced
1/4 cup butter
1/2 cup grated Parmesan cheese

Melt 1/4 cup of the butter in a large skillet. Add the peas and sweet peppers and sauté for about 3 minutes. Add the cream and bring to a slow boil. Cook until the sauce is reduced by about one-quarter. Add the tomatoes and cook for 10 minutes. Place hot pasta in a heated serving bowl. Add the remaining 1/4 cup butter and Parmesan cheese. Toss to mix. Pour the hot sauce over and toss again. Serve immediately. Serves 4 to 6.

Asparagus and Porcini Cream

This sauce works well with penne or rotelli.

1/2 ounce dried porcini mushrooms
1/2 cup water
1/2 pound asparagus, washed, trimmed, and
cut into l-inch lengths (or same
lengths as the pasta)
1 cup heavy cream
2 teaspoons fresh lemon juice
salt and freshly ground ground black pepper

Combine the porcini mushrooms and water in a small saucepan. Heat to boiling and simmer, covered, for 5 minutes. Let stand, off heat, for 10 minutes. Strain the liquid through a fine sieve or a sieve lined with a piece of dampened cheesecloth; reserve the liquid. Rinse mushrooms, checking carefully for grit. Finely chop mushrooms and set aside.

Meanwhile, steam the asparagus on a steaming rack set over 1 inch of boiling water, covered, until crisp-tender, about 5 minutes. Remove asparagus from pan and set aside. Combine the cream, porcini liquid, and the chopped porcini in a deep sauce pan. Heat to boiling, stirring occasionally, until liquid is reduced to 2/3 cup, about 10 minutes. Add asparagus, lemon juice and salt and pepper to taste. Toss with hot pasta. Serves 4.

Tomato-Raisin Anchovy Sauce

This unusual combination of sweet and salty ingredients makes a great topping for rigatoni.

**3 tablespoons olive oil
1 tablespoon minced garlic
1 tablespoon minced anchovies
1 (14 ounce) can Italian-style plum tomatoes,
with juice, cut up with scissors
1 tablespoon raisins or dried currants
1 tablespoon chopped Italian flat-leaf parsley
freshly ground black pepper to taste
1 tablespoon pignoli (pine nuts), stirred in a hot
skillet until lightly toasted, 1 to 2 minutes**

Heat oil in a medium skillet. Stir in garlic and anchovies. Sauté, stirring, over low heat until anchovies dissolve completely. Stir in the tomatoes and raisins. Heat to boiling, stirring and mashing tomatoes. Simmer, uncovered, 10 minutes, or until slightly thickened. Stir in parsley and season with pepper to taste. Toss with hot pasta and sprinkle with pignoli. Serves 4.

Roasted Peppers and Olives

The peppers make a wonderful appetizer on their own or serve over pasta for a main course.

4 large sweet red bell peppers
1/2 cup olive oil
2 tablespoons tiny imported black olives, pitted
1 garlic clove, bruised
1 tablespoon whole fresh oregano leaves
salt and freshly ground black pepper to taste
2 tablespoons pignoli (pine nuts), lightly toasted
freshly grated Parmesan cheese
sprigs of fresh oregano, if available

Place the peppers in a baking pan lined with foil; broil about 3 inches from the heat until well charred on all sides. Cover with a towel and let stand until cool. Carefully peel off the charred skin, working over the foil to reserve all of the pepper juices. Split the peppers in half and remove seeds and stems. Rinse under running water. Cut the peppers in 1/2-inch strips and place in a shallow bowl. Drain the skins and seeds in the foil through a sieve and pour juices over the peeled peppers. Add the oil, olives, garlic, oregano, salt, and pepper. Cover and marinate at room temperature 1 to 2 hours, or refrigerate overnight. Bring marinated peppers to room temperature before serving, if refrigerated. Remove the garlic clove. Toss hot pasta with the marinated peppers. Garnish with the pignoli, Parmesan, and oregano. Serves 4.

Fresh Artichoke Sauce

Tiny artichokes, usually less than 2 inches in length, are usually available in September and then again in April. Although frozen artichokes can be used, fresh ones are delectable.

16 tiny fresh artichokes
Juice of 1 lemon
1/3 cup olive oil
1/2 cup coarsely chopped Spanish onion
3 garlic cloves, peeled and crushed
1 medium carrot, pared and sliced thin
1 stalk celery, trimmed and sliced thin
1/2 teaspoon dried oregano
salt and freshly ground black pepper to taste
1 (14 ounce) can Italian plum tomatoes with juices

Trim the stems and pull all the outside leaves off the artichokes. Cut the artichokes in half; scoop out the choke with the tip of a small spoon or knife. Halve lengthwise. Add the lemon juice to a bowl of water; add the artichokes to prevent darkening. In a sauté pan, combine the oil, onion, garlic, carrot, and celery. Cover and cook over low heat, stirring occasionally for 5 minutes. Drain the artichokes and add to the pan. Stir to coat. Cover and cook over low heat, stirring occasionally, until artichokes are tender, about 25 minutes. Season with salt, oregano, and pepper. Stir in the tomatoes and cook, uncovered, until the liquid is slightly reduced, about 10 minutes Toss with hot pasta. Serves 4.

Bacon, Mushrooms, and Pignoli

This simple recipe served over farfelle (butterflies) or rotelli makes a great side dish for grilled steak or chicken.

4 ounces thick-sliced bacon, cut into 2-inch lengths
2 tablespoons pignoli (pine nuts)
2 tablespoons butter
2 tablespoons olive oil
6 ounces small mushrooms, trimmed and quartered
salt and freshly ground black pepper to taste
1 scallion, trimmed and sliced

Sauté bacon in a medium skillet until crisp. Transfer to a double thickness of paper towels to drain. Spoon off and discard all but 1 tablespoon of the bacon fat from the pan. Add the pignoli and sauté, stirring, until golden. Transfer to the paper towels with the bacon.

Heat the butter and oil in the same skillet. Then add the mushrooms and sauté over moderately high heat, stirring, until the mushroom liquid cooks off and the mushrooms begin to brown. Stir in the reserved bacon and pignoli. Season with salt and pepper to taste. Toss hot pasta with the bacon and mushroom mixture and the scallion. Serves 4.

Spicy Vegetable Sauce

In the mood for something light and fresh? Try a peppery blend of vegetables over spinach fusilli or penne.

2 tablespoons olive oil
2 tablespoons butter
1 cup each julienned carrots, onions, zucchini
and yellow squash
1 garlic clove, minced
1/4 teaspoon white pepper
1/4 teaspoon cayenne pepper
1/2 teaspoon each paprika, black pepper
and dried oregano
2 tablespoons flour
2/3 cup dry white wine
1/2 cup water
juice of 1 lemon
2 medium-size fresh Italian plum tomatoes,
halved and sliced

Heat the oil and butter in a large saucepan over medium heat. Add the carrots, onions, and garlic and sauté for 3 minutes. Add the zucchini, yellow squash, and spices. Continue to sauté for 3 minutes. Reduce the heat to medium low and stir in the flour, blending it into the vegetables. Slowly add the wine and water, stirring constantly until the sauce has thickened. Add the lemon juice and tomatoes. Slowly cook for 5 more minutes. Serve over hot pasta. Serves 4.

Potatoes, Broccoli, and Red Pepper

6 tablespoons olive oil
1 small red bell pepper, seeded, cut into thin strips
1/2 teaspoon crushed dried red pepper
1 small garlic clove, cut into thin slivers
3 cups cubed (1/2-inch) unpared new potatoes
3 cups broccoli florets,
cut into approximately 1/2-inch pieces
freshly grated Parmesan cheese

Heat oil in a medium skillet. Add bell pepper and sauté 3 minutes, or until crisp-tender. Add the crushed red pepper and garlic and sauté 1 minute more. Cook potatoes and broccoli in a medium saucepan in about 1 inch of lightly salted water. Steam until they are tender, about 8 minutes. Drain and toss with the peppers and plenty of freshly grated Parmesan cheese. Toss with hot pasta. Pass with more Parmesan. Serves 4.

Fennel and Sun-Dried Tomato Sauce

Wonderful little oval-shaped "pasta pillows" or cavatelli are the perfect compliment to this sauce. Try to find them fresh or frozen.

**1/4 cup olive oil
1 cup finely chopped fresh fennel
(save tops when trimming)
2 tablespoons minced onion
1 (14 ounce) can Italian-style plum tomatoes
with juice, chopped
1/4 cup minced, drained, and
blotted sun-dried tomatoes, packed in oil
2 tablespoons fennel tops, finely chopped
(fernlike tops saved from fennel)
salt and freshly ground black pepper to taste**

Heat the oil in a medium skillet. Add the fennel and onion. Sauté, stirring, over low heat until the fennel is very soft but not browned, about 15 minutes. Add the plum tomatoes; cook, stirring and crushing tomatoes, with the side of a spoon, until juices are slightly reduced and the sauce is thickened, about 15 minutes. Add the sun-dried tomatoes and fennel tops. Simmer over low heat 5 minutes. Season with salt and pepper to taste. Toss with hot pasta. Serves 4.

Lima Beans and Sun-Dried Tomatoes

Try this sauce with farfalle,which correctly translated in Italian means butterfly.

6 tablespoons olive oil
1/2 cup coarsely chopped onion
8 sun-dried tomato halves packed in olive oil,
blotted and cut into thin slices
1 garlic clove, minced
1 (10 ounce) package frozen Fordhook lima beans
freshly ground black pepper to taste

Heat oil in a medium skillet. Add the onion and sauté until golden. Stir in the tomatoes and garlic; set aside.

Meanwhile, cook pasta in plenty of boiling salted water about 3 minutes, Add the lima beans and cook until the pasta is al dente, or firm to the bite, and the lima beans are tender. Drain and toss the oil mixture and the pasta mixture together until blended. Season with freshly ground black pepper. Serves 4.

Eggplant and Olive Sauce

This sauce was inspired by a Sicilian eggplant appetizer called caponata. It is especially good with penne or ziti.

6 tablespoons olive oil
1 small (about 1 pound) eggplant, trimmed, pared, and cut into 1/2-inch chunks
1 cup chopped onion
1/2 cup chopped green pepper
1/2 cup chopped celery
1 cup chopped fresh tomatoes
1/4 cup chopped crushed green olives
1 tablespoon rinsed and drained small capers
1 tablespoon chopped fresh basil
1 tablespoon chopped Italian flat-leaf parsley
2 teaspoons red wine vinegar
1/2 teaspoon salt
freshly ground black pepper to taste
Pinch of sugar

Heat 4 tablespoons of the oil in a large skillet over high heat; add the eggplant. Sauté, stirring constantly, until eggplant is tender and browned. Transfer to a plate lined with paper towels to drain. Add remaining 2 tablespoons oil to skillet. Add onion, green pepper and celery, and sauté stirring until tender, about 5 minutes. Stir in the eggplant, tomatoes, olives, capers, basil, parsley, vinegar, salt, pepper, and sugar. Cover and simmer 5 minutes. Toss hot pasta with the sauce. Serves 4.

Yogurt Herb Sauce

For an interesting visual effect try serving over a combination of red and green pasta rotelli.

1/2 ounce butter
1 small onion, chopped
1 clove garlic, crushed
2 tablespoons flour
1/2 cup vegetable stock
1-3/4 cups natural yogurt
2 tablespoons fresh parsley, finely chopped
2 tablespoons fresh basil, finely chopped
2 tablespoons snipped fresh chives
freshly ground black pepper

Melt butter in a saucepan and cook onion and garlic over a medium heat for 2 to 3 minutes. Stir in flour and vegetable stock and cook, stirring constantly, for an additional 4 to 5 minutes or until sauce boils and thickens. Remove from heat, stir in yogurt and simmer over a low heat for 2 to 3 minutes longer. Mix in parsley, basil and chives and season to taste with black pepper. Spoon over pasta and serve immediately. Serves 4.

Lemony Chicken Zucchini Sauce

A light, zesty sauce with colorful flecks of green from the zucchini. Serve over linguine or shells.

1/4 cup olive oil
5 large garlic cloves, minced
2 whole boneless chicken breasts,
cut into 2-inch strips
2-1/2 tablespoons flour
1 cup dry white wine
1 cup chicken broth
juice of 1 lemon
1 cup coarsely grated zucchini, firmly packed
4 scallions, including green tops, sliced
salt and freshly ground black pepper to taste
1 teaspoon dried summer savory

Heat the oil in a large skillet over medium high heat. Add the garlic and chicken and sauté for 4 minutes. Sprinkle the flour over the chicken and mix well. Reduce the heat to medium and add the wine, chicken broth, and lemon juice. Cook, stirring constantly, until the sauce thickens. Stir in the zucchini, scallions, salt and black pepper, and summer savory and heat through. Serve over hot pasta Serves 4.

Chicken Artichoke Sauce

3 tablespoons olive oil
1 pound chicken breast, skin removed
and cut into strips
1/2 cup chopped shallots
2 tablespoons flour
1-1/2 cups chicken broth
1 cup dry white wine
2 tablespoons capers, drained
1 tablespoon lemon juice
freshly ground black pepper to taste
1 (14-ounce) can artichoke hearts,
drained and cut into quarters
1/4 pound snowpeas, cut into thin slivers

In a medium-size skillet, heat the oil over medium-high heat. Add the chicken and sauté until the chicken is lightly brown. Reduce the heat to medium-low and add the shallots. Sauté for 2 minutes. Sprinkle the flour over the chicken and shallots, stirring constantly until the flour is well blended. Add the chicken broth and wine. Cook, stirring, until the sauce has thickened. Add the capers, lemon juice, pepper, artichokes, and snowpeas and cook for about 3 minutes. Serve over hot pasta. Serves 4.

Salmon with Asparagus & Lemon Butter

2 salmon steaks, each about 8 ounces
1 teaspoon soy sauce
1/2 pound asparagus, trimmed, stems peeled, cut
into diagonals about 2 inches long
6 tablespoons butter
1 clove garlic
1/2 teaspoon grated fresh ginger
1 tablespoon fresh lemon juice
1 tablespoon grated lemon zest

Brush the salmon steak lightly on both sides with the soy. Grill or broil until almost cooked through, about 3 minutes a side for a steak 1/2-inch thick. Cool slightly; remove and discard outside skin and center bone. Pull salmon into large flakes.

Steam the asparagus, covered, on a steaming rack set over 1 inch of simmering water until crisp-tender, about 4 minutes. Transfer to a plate; cover to keep warm. Melt the butter in a saucepan and add the garlic and ginger; sauté 30 seconds. Add the lemon juice and zest. Toss the hot pasta, asparagus, and melted butter until pasta is coated. Add the salmon and gently toss. Serves 4.

Chapter 6

Fast and Easy Sauces

Arugula and Garlic Sauce

Arugula is a green vegetable that is also known as rocket or raquette. It has a peppery taste that blends well with tomatoes. Use this pasta preparation as a side dish to go with a meat main course.

2 tablespoons olive oil
2 tablespoons butter
1/2 red onion, cut into thin lengthwise slices
2 garlic cloves, minced
1 bunch arugula, rinsed and trimmed,
about 1 cup packed
salt and freshly ground black pepper to taste

Heat oil and butter in a medium skillet over low heat; stir in red onion; saute until crisp-tender, about 3 minutes. Stir in garlic; saute 1 minute. Add the arugula; saute, stirring, about 2 minutes. Season with salt and pepper. Toss hot pasta with the sauce. Serves 4.

Easy Primavera Sauce

This quick and easy version of Primavera Sauce still goes best over the traditional fettuccine.

2 tablespoons butter
1 (16 ounce) bag frozen Italian-style vegetables
(contains zucchini, cauliflower, lima beans, carrots,
and green beans)
1 egg
1/3 cup heavy cream
1/2 cup freshly grated Parmesan cheese
1/2 basket cherry tomatoes, rinsed
1 tablespoon chopped Italian flat-leaf parsley

Melt butter in a wide skillet then stir in vegetables. Cook, stirring, over low heat until tender, about 5 minutes. Beat egg, cream, and Parmesan cheese in a serving bowl. Add hot pasta to the bowl with the cream mixture; toss to coat. Add the vegetables, cherry tomatoes, and parsley; toss and serve. Serves 2 to 4.

Zucchini, Mushroom, and Fresh Tomato Sauce

Mushroom powder and Canadian bacon give this full-flavored sauce a slightly smokey hint. It goes well with tagliatelli or fettuccine.

2 tablespoons olive oil
1 cup diced trimmed mushrooms
1/3 cup chopped scallions, some tops included
2 cups finely diced trimmed zucchini
4 (1/4-inch-thick) slices of Canadian bacon,
cut into thin strips
1 garlic clove, crushed
1 cup chopped fresh tomatoes
1 cup dry red wine
1 tablespoon mushroom powder
1/4 cup chopped Italian flat-leaf parsley
2 tablespoons chopped fresh basil
salt and freshly grated black pepper
freshly grated Parmesan cheese

Heat oil in a wide saucepan. Add mushrooms and sauté 4 minutes. Stir in scallions, zucchini, Canadian bacon and garlic and sauté over medium high heat, stirring, until tender, about 8 minutes. Add tomatoes, wine and mushroom powder; cook, stirring, 5 minutes. Add parsley, basil, salt and pepper. Toss with hot pasta. Pass with freshly grated Parmesan cheese, if desired. Serves 4 to 6.

Summer Garden Sauce

This sauce, perfect for a late August supper, is especially good on penne, ziti, or fusilli.

5 tablespoons olive oil
1 cup chopped Spanish onion
1 medium red bell pepper, stems and seeds removed, diced
1 medium green bell pepper, stems and seeds removed, diced
1 small eggplant (about 1 pound), trimmed, peeled, and cut into 1/2-inch cubes
1 pound fresh ripe tomatoes, cored and diced
1 garlic clove, crushed
1 teaspoon salt
1/4 teaspoon black pepper
2 tablespoons chopped fresh basil
Grated Parmesan cheese

Heat olive oil in a large, heavy, preferably nonstick skillet. Add onion and red and green peppers; saute until tender, about 10 minutes. Add eggplant; cook over high heat stirring frequently until eggplant begins to brown about 5 minutes. Stir in tomatoes, garlic, salt, and pepper. Cook, stirring, 5 minutes. Stir in basil. Toss hot pasta with the sauce and serve at once. Serve with cheese, if desired. Serves 4.

Herbed Red Pepper Sauce

3 medium-size sweet red peppers
2 tablespoons olive oil
1 tablespoon butter
1/4 cup chopped garlic
1 cup chopped onion
3/4 cup very finely diced carrots
2 cups chopped mushrooms
1/4 cup minced fresh herbs (a combination of
thyme, savory, oregano is recommended)
1/2 cup chicken stock or broth
1/2 cup chopped fresh parsley
salt and freshly ground pepper to taste

Place the peppers in a baking pan lined with foil; broil about 3 inches from the heat until well charred on all sides. Cover with a towel and let stand until cool. Carefully peel off the charred skin. Peel the stem away, removing the seeds and veins. Roughly chop the peppers. You should have about 1 cup chopped roasted red peppers.

Heat the oil and butter in a large skillet and add the garlic, onion, and carrots. Sauté until the vegetables are softened, 2 to 3 minutes. Add the chopped red peppers, mushrooms, herbs, and chicken stock. Simmer gently, stirring frequently, until the sauce has reduced by half. Fold in the parsley. Season with salt and pepper. Toss with hot pasta. Pass with freshly grated Parmesan cheese. Serves 4.

Tomato, Sardine, and Green Bean Sauce

This crunchy sauce mixes well with shells.

1/4 cup olive oil
1/2 cup chopped onion
1 cup trimmed and cut-up green beans (1/2 inch)
1 clove garlic, crushed
1 cup chopped fresh tomatoes
1 teaspoon grated orange zest
1 (3-3/4 ounce) can sardines in olive oil, drained
2 tablespoons chopped Italian flat-leaf parsley
2 tablespoons chopped fresh basil
salt and freshly ground black pepper to taste

Heat oil in a large skillet. Add onion and sauté 5 minutes. Stir in green beans and sauté over low heat until crisp-tender, about 5 minutes. Stir in garlic; sauté 1 minute. Add tomatoes and orange zest. Simmer 10 minutes, or until sauce is slightly thickened. Add sardines, parsley, and basil; stir gently. Add salt and pepper to taste. Toss with hot pasta. Serves 4.

Marinated Mushroom Sauce

This sauce combined with rotelli or shells can be served as an appetizer or can be mixed with cold pasta and served as a salad.

1/2 pound small white mushrooms, coarsely chopped
1/4 cup finely chopped red onion
1/4 cup finely chopped red bell pepper
1/4 cup chopped Italian flat-leaf parsley
1 tablespoon fresh oregano leaves
OR 1/2 teaspoon dried
1 teaspoon fresh thyme leaves
OR 1/4 teaspoon dried
1/3 cup olive oil
2 tablespoons fresh lemon juice
salt and freshly ground black pepper to taste

Combine the mushrooms, onion, red pepper, parsley, oregano, and thyme in a small bowl. Whisk the oil, lemon juice, salt, and pepper in a separate bowl; fold together. Cover and marinate, refrigerated, 1 to 2 hours. Toss sauce with hot pasta and serve at once. Serves 4.

Fresh Tomato Sauce with Ricotta

Try this rich sauce with rigatoni, penne, or ridged ziti.

2 tablespoons olive oil
1 garlic clove, crushed
1-1/2 cups chopped fresh ripe tomatoes
(about 1 pound)
2 tablespoons chopped fresh basil
1 tablespoon chopped Italian flat-leaf parsley
1/2 teaspoon fresh oregano leaves (optional)
1/4 teaspoon fresh thyme leaves (optional)
1 cup whole milk ricotta cheese
salt and freshly ground black pepper
freshly grated Parmesan cheese

Heat oil in a medium skillet over low heat. Stir in garlic; sauté 1 minute. Add tomatoes. Simmer, uncovered, until mixture boils and begins to thicken, about 10 minutes. Add basil, parsley, oregano, and thyme; whisk in ricotta until blended. Heat, stirring, about 1 minute. Add salt and pepper. Toss hot pasta with the sauce. Pass with freshly grated Parmesan cheese. Serves 4.

Zucchini, Carrot and Parmesan Sauce

This brightly colored sauce is good on twists, rotelli, or any pasta that will "catch" the sauce. Shred the vegetables in a food processor or on the widest side of a hand grater.

1/3 cup olive oil
2 garlic cloves, crushed
1-1/2 cups shredded carrot
1-1/2 cups shredded trimmed zucchini
freshly grated Parmesan cheese

Heat the oil over low heat in a medium skillet. Stir in the carrot, zucchini, and garlic. Sauté, stirring, for 3 minutes. Toss hot pasta with the sauce. Pass with freshly grated Parmesan cheese. Serves 4.

Chapter 7

No-Cook
Sauces
for Hot Pasta

Artichoke and Sun-Dried Tomato Sauce

This no-cook sauce for hot pasta can be served over penne, medium shells, or twists.

**1 (6 ounce) jar marinated artichokes,
rinsed, well drained, and chopped
1 (7 ounce) jar roasted red peppers,
rinsed, well drained, and chopped
1/4 cup chopped Italian flat-leaf parsley
2 tablespoons minced sundried tomatoes
in oil, well drained
1 tablespoon pitted and slivered
brine-cured black olives
1/2 cup olive oil
1 tablespoon red wine vinegar
1 garlic clove, crushed
1/8 teaspoon freshly ground black pepper**

Combine all ingredients in a small bowl. Stir well to blend. Toss hot pasta with sauce and serve. Serves 4.

Tuna, Artichoke and Olive Sauce

Serve over angel hair for a quick lunch.

**1/2 cup chopped marinated artichoke hearts
1 (6-1/2 ounce) can imported Italian tuna
in olive oil, rinsed and drained
1/2 cup olive oil
2 tablespoons chopped Italian flat-leaf parsley
1 tablespoon pitted and chopped
imported black olives
1 garlic clove, crushed**

Combine all the ingredients in a bowl; stir to blend. Toss hot pasta with the sauce and serve at once. Serves 4.

Tomato, Onion and Sardine Sauce

This sauce works well as a side dish and serves well over spaghetti or linguine.

2 cups finely chopped fresh tomatoes
1/2 cup red onion, chopped
1/2 cup scallions, chopped including some tops
1/4 cup finely chopped red flat-leaf parsley
1/4 cup olive oil
1 tablespoon fresh lemon juice
1 garlic clove, crushed
salt and freshly ground black pepper to taste
1 (3-3/4 ounce) can imported sardines
packed in water, drained

Combine the tomatoes, red onion, scallions, parsley, olive oil, lemon juice garlic, salt and pepper in a bowl. Toss hot pasta with sauce and serve at once. Serves 4.

Fresh and Sun-Dried Tomato Sauce

2 cups chopped ripe tomatoes
1/2 cup thinly sliced scallions
1/4 cup drained and chopped sun-dried
tomatoes in olive oil
1/4 cup chopped fresh basil
1/4 cup chopped Italian flat-leaf parsley
2 garlic cloves, crushed
salt and freshly ground black pepper to taste
1/2 cup olive oil

Combine the fresh tomatoes, scallions, sun-dried tomatoes, basil, parsley, garlic, salt, and pepper. Stir in the oil. Toss sauce with hot pasta and serve at once. Serves 4.

Tricolor Tomato Sauce with Mint

This is an especially pretty sauce if yellow tomatoes are available. The tomato adds a pleasant astringency that is nicely balanced by the mint Serve with fusilli, small shells, or tubetti.

1 cup chopped ripe red tomatoes
1 cup chopped yellow tomatoes
1/4 cup minced green tomato
1/4 cup olive oil
2 tablespoons finely chopped parsley
2 tablespoons finely chopped fresh mint
1 garlic clove, crushed
1/8 teaspoon coarsely ground black pepper

Stir all the ingredients together in a bowl. Toss hot pasta with the sauce and serve at once. Serves 4.

Roasted Red Pepper and Ricotta Sauce

This easy-to-make sauce goes best with spaghetti or medium-size grooved pasta, such as radiatore, fusilli, or shells.

**1 (15 ounce) container whole milk ricotta cheese
1 (7 ounce) jar roasted red peppers,
rinsed and well drained
1/4 cup olive oil
1 tablespoon grated Parmesan cheese
1 garlic clove, crushed
2 tablespoons chopped Italian flat-leaf parsley
1 teaspoon fresh oregano leaves
OR 1/4 teaspoon dried oregano**

Pureé ricotta, roasted red peppers, oil, Parmesan cheese, and garlic in the bowl of a food processor. Stir in parsley and oregano. Toss sauce with hot pasta and serve at once. Serves 4.

Yellow Tomato and Cilantro Sauce

Yellow tomatoes are very delicately flavored, allowing the flavor of other ingredients to be tasted. They go well with cilantro, which has a distinctively sharp, smokey flavor.

1-1/2 cups chopped yellow tomato
1/2 cup coarsely shredded, peeled
and seeded cucumber
2 tablespoons minced red bell pepper
1 tablespoon chopped fresh basil
1 tablespoon chopped fresh cilantro
1 teaspoon minced, seeded hot chili pepper,
or to taste
1 scallion, trimmed and sliced very thin
6 tablespoons olive oil
3 tablespoons fresh lime juice
1/2 teaspoon salt, or to taste
1 garlic clove, crushed

Combine the yellow tomato, cucumber, red bell pepper, basil, cilantro, chili pepper, and scallion. Add the oil, lime juice, salt, and garlic; toss to blend. Toss hot pasta with the sauce and serve at once. Serves 4

Fresh From the Garden Sauce

If you have a garden this is a fast way to serve up a delicious meal from your vegetable harvest. Serve with rotelli or shells.

1-1/2 cups chopped ripe tomatoes
1/4 cup diced peeled cucumber
1/4 cup chopped seeded green bell pepper
1/4 cup chopped trimmed zucchini
1/4 cup chopped scallions
1 ear corn, husked, kernels cut from the cob
(uncooked), about 1/2 cup
1 medium carrot, peeled and coarsely shredded
1/4 cup finely chopped fresh parsley
1/4 cup finely chopped fresh basil
2 tablespoons diced radishes
6 tablespoons olive oil
1 tablespoon red wine vinegar
1 garlic clove, crushed
1/2 teaspoon salt, or to taste
freshly ground black pepper to taste

Combine the tomatoes, cucumber, green pepper, zucchini, scallions, corn, carrot, parsley, basil, and radishes. Add the oil, vinegar, garlic, salt, and pepper; toss to blend. Let stand, covered, 20 minutes before using. This sauce can be made ahead and refrigerated, but should be eaten the same day as made. Toss sauce with hot pasta and serve at once. Serves 4.